Enigma

Brooke Fancy

BookLeaf Publishing

Presentation by *BookLeaf Publishing*

Web: www.bookleafpub.com

E-mail: info@bookleafpub.com

ISBN: 9789357616935

First edition 2022

Dedicated to the wallflowers, outcasts, weirdos and to anyone's hands that happen to come across this book, for whatever reason.

Poem 1

I always
told you that
one day
I'd get better
I guess
Later is better
than never

I don't want to live
in a world
without you in it
I said I wouldn't
move on
from you
And
I didn't.

Avalanche

I try to talk
to you
But it's hard
When I know you
won't understand
you'll simply
not comprehend
the magnitude
the limits the mind can reach
are limitless…
almost.

It's So Unusual
You're gone but
It's like
I'm becoming you
or so it seems.
Your facial expressions
And all those things
you would do
God I hate myself
When you left
Things changed
faster than I could ever imagine
Everything.

Like life was an avalanche
and now that you're gone
it's filling in all the space you left behind
Tangled, mauled and mixed
Filling the cracks and craters
However it does
And it does.
Life goes on.

30 000 Ft

I'm drinking this cheap red wine
Passing the time
As I'm
30,000 ft in the sky
The clouds drift by
Thinking about how
I never got to say goodbye

A Haiku

Those Smokey quartz eyes
Burned my brain like a branding
Hard to stay away

You

I like you.

You're crazy just as I am.
I know you're reading this
Thinking it's about you
Maybe you won't think I'm fun anymore
I can barely stand to drink
These days
I stopped taking my anti-depressants
I know you'd be proud of that
But my anxiety gets so bad now
After a night of drinking
That I avoid it if possible
My anxiety also gets bad for
no reason at all
At least when I drink
For a little
I feel invincible
I know you're jealous
Because I never relied on drugs
To be spiritual
And to expand my consciousness
and mind
I can feel the silence getting louder
I don't care if I'm crazy

I’d rather be that than
Anything like them
I know you get that
I know you always spoke so highly of me
And saw my potential
But
I don't think there's any hope for me anymore

I'm too far gone.

Us

We're slow dancing to songs
That speak to our souls
For some reason
Drunk off of the cheapest wine
We could find
Just us
Wrapped up in each other
Intertwined
I miss those days
More than I'd ever say
We're both crazy
In our own ways
The best people
always are
I've lost my mind
And it is clear that
You can't find yours either
But we're more alike than we want to admit
No one else gets us
No one gets me like you do
It always ends with us again
Staring at the stars
Is it all even real
Nothing else matters but this moment
And even this moment doesn't matter

In the grand scheme of things
But I’d rather be here with you
Than alone tonight
you distract me from my mind
And sometimes
That’s all I really need.
You’re like my God.
We're God's
No one else sees the world
As closely to the way I do
And even if there’s others
I don’t care enough to seek them out
Some things are just meant to be
Why try and change it

If it’s not worth writing about
Then it’s simply not worth it all

Anxiety

My anxiety
Gets the best of me
Debilitating
She's rude.
She's shy.
She's dumb.
No
I'm just stuck in my mind
Trapped.

Wasted Time

Now I gotta spend all of my time
Making up for wasted time
God, let me relive my youth

Wasting time
making up for wasted time
I feel so alone
Like no one could understand me
Like they won't even try

Me

But you know me
I'm beyond help
And you're better off
Staying far away from
wherever I am
But still
Love me till
The only beautiful thing left
Are these pretty little
Words I put on paper

Enigma

Enigma,
It fills people up
When they understand you
Although, they rarely do
How would they when
You don't even understand yourself?

Nothing has ever felt right
Or meant to be or
Permanent
You're always ready to run
To flee, to hide
They say it's just social anxiety
That's part of it
Crippling, anxiety
But there's more to it
The only time you feel free
Is when you're in nature
swimming in the sea
How you live most of the time
It's no way to be
But you've been this way for so long
And everyone is aware of how
Hard it is to change
It drains you trying to explain

yourself to people
Who will never get it
So now you try not to care
And just live for yourself
There has to be more than this
Oh, Enigma!
And if there isn't then what's the point?
What's the point to change, to try
You don't even cry anymore
Because nothings worth the effort
You have loved, hated
Lost and regret
Grieved and tried and failed to forget
nightmares,
But every day awake is just the same
Not being able to deal with the trivialities
anymore
Not caring about most of what society has to
offer
Or most of what people talk about
You don't want to live this way
Or be associated with these people and their
ways
And what they care about or praise
you wish you could spend your days
Outside of it all
Outside, with nature
Less possessions
Not striving for this materialistic

Goal that is bullshit and doesn't matter
Because when you're in the grave
Or turned to dust
It wont matter what you owned
It shouldn't even matter
While you're alive
We own nothing
Not even our own bodies
Which will return to the dirt
No matter what we have to say about it
it's all so pointless
But as beautiful and metaphorical
As a rose, so beautiful, in every way
Blooms for just a moment
Just to whither away for eternity
Enigma
All you have is this thought that life, and those moments are a work of art
Something so beautiful
So impermanent
That it slips away in the middle of the night
And will forever be a memory
Until you're gone and
The memory is no longer
We should live being fully aware
Of the impermanence of it all
And love the same way.

Soulmate?

I love your soul
I love that you're different
You know how to love me
Just like I need
I love how you say
No one
Deserves it but me

6 Feet Down

You still have 5 fingers around my neck
And I still have those feelings 4 you
It's 3AM and I just want to be free
Free like what you wanted 2 be
But I can't help thinking
you were the 1

The power you hold
Even after your death

Feline

Me and my cat
We have our own language
She understands me
And I get her
She's very timid
Scared.
It's hard for her to trust.
She even gets scared of me
Sometimes
If I move too fast or raise my voice.
We are the same.

Prom Queen

Prom queen
Just eighteen
Red and blue
Me and you
What is love
We thought it was true
Little did we know
We never knew
It almost seems silly now
Or was that true love
The fog blocking reality
Make love till the AM
While listening to the album
You told me you
Never seen someone look pretty
When they cry
Then you said bye
And you understood
I just didn’t know how to act
But I mean that was ten years ago
It’s pretty blurry looking back
Has your hand writing gotten any better?
I remember it was a pain to read your letters
I don't even care anymore
It doesn’t hurt anymore

I just thought it was all
worth one poem
I'm glad you found happiness
And I wish you the best
Nothing less

Gone

You're gone
But I am still here
More here than I've ever been
Yet so lost
I'm so aware of
How lost
I am.
How gone you are.
It's so wrong
I don't know what to do
Anymore

I miss you

I miss you
When I see
glimpses
Of you in him
Or in myself or
In daily life

I miss you
I know I shouldn't
I should let the feelings
and the memories die
Like you did
But they seem to
Want to live on inside
My head

I miss you
No one understands me
Like you did
No one tries
Like you did
It's just not right
To live on a planet
Where you are not

The feeling of
Your eyes
Looking into mine
The way our lips
Stuck together
There is no name
For this type of pain

I'm sorry and I love you

Pending

My gut tells me it's wrong
But I don't know
What's real anymore
My judgement is so clouded
I may just be crazy
I don't know how
I'm supposed to act
In society
In a relationship
I don't know when something
Is bad or good
Real or fake
I know
We live together
But love doesn't live here

Phantom

You're gone
But haunt me everyday
You're the songs that come on the radio

You're bits and pieces of myself
A teardrop that runs down my cheeks
You're the unexpressed emotions
Unanswered questions
Guilt and grief
That are trapped inside
That I'm forced to hide

Nothing stings quite like regret.

You left with the Spring
And made the Summer so cold

Don't Try.

I don’t even want to try
If this is all there is
Sometimes it hurts
To just be alive
I don’t care enough to try
I’m not gonna lie
I find these days I can’t even
Manage to do the bare minimum
People call it lazy
From what they see on the surface
I call it being trapped
They call me crazy
Trapped in my bad habits
Trapped in my mind, my anxiety
Maybe I deserve this

I feel peace in a quiet room
Door shut, locked, cut off from everything
Just me and my cat
Pure Bliss.
No one thing to expel energy into
No putting on a front.
I don’t even know what they
Want from me anymore.
I just want to be loved.

I’d much rather, say nothing
Do nothing.
Be nothing.
In an infinite universe, full of mysteries
We came to be on this rock
And they want to talk about the
Trivialities
It is the most unpoetic thing imaginable
But some how
I still talk about it in these poems

I have started to try and take
My health more seriously
Because i feel myself disintegrating
Slowly but surely
Hopefully it'll benefit my mind too
I get worried sometimes
That I just can't take much more
Of this Hell
That is myself
There's not much good
Or motivation
Or reason
To continue in
It seems
Everything sucks
But I'll just keep
Drinking water
Doing Pilates

Hoping for a revelation

Nowadays
Everything is mediocre and disappointing
And I just accept it
Because at this point
Okay the god complex has faded
And I realize
This is either my destiny
Or
It is the result of what I've manifested
It is what I deserve
It's probably both
It also doesn't matter

Every day is just the same
Living not knowing what to do
Dehabilitated by my anxiety
Stuck
Trying to conquer the smallest
Trivialities of life
So I can move on to whatever matters
Whatever that it is
Where do I go
I thought I was good or clever at writing
But now that I'm writing this
Poetry book
I don't even know about that

Imagine

Imagine all the poetry
That would exist
That will never exist
If I would have
Been writing
During all those miserable times
I could try and recreate it
And I do
But it could never compete
To writing while you're living it

Queen of Free Verse

I often feel anxious
To write the right thing
So I simply write what's real
I write what I feel
Sometimes I just need more hurt
More inspiration to get it right
Never did like rules
Why would it be different
Maybe I'll be an elite poet one day
When I learn better words
Go through a couple more tragedies
Read some more Bukowski
Being a poet is the best option for the song
writer who can't sing for shit